BORDERS, FRAMES & DECORATIONS OF THE ART NOUVEAU PERIOD

Edited by
Carol Belanger Grafton

DOVER PUBLICATIONS, INC., New York

Copyright © 1984 by Dover Publications, Inc.
All rights reserved under Pan American and International Copyright Conventions.

Published in Canada by General Publishing Company, Ltd., 30 Lesmill Road, Don Mills,
Toronto, Ontario.
Published in the United Kingdom by Constable and Company, Ltd.

Borders, Frames and Decorations of the Art Nouveau Period is a new work, first published by Dover Publications, Inc., in 1984. The selection and arrangement of illustrations,
from *Jugend: Die Münchner illustrierte Wochenschrift für Kunst und Leben*, Volumes I–
XVIII (Georg Hirth, Munich, 1896–1913), are by Carol Belanger Grafton. The Publisher's
Note and Index of Artists were prepared specially for this edition.

DOVER *Pictorial Archive* SERIES

Manufactured in the United States of America
Dover Publications, Inc., 31 East 2nd Street, Mineola, N.Y. 11501

Library of Congress Cataloging in Publication Data
Main entry under title:

Border, frames and decorations of the art nouveau period.

(Dover pictorial archive series)
Illustrations selected and arranged from Jugend, v. 1-18 (1896-1913)
Includes index.
1. Borders, Ornamental (Decorative arts) 2. Decoration and ornament—Art nouveau.
I. Grafton, Carol Belanger. II. Jugend (Munich, Germany) III. Series.
NK3630.4.B67B67 1984   745.4'441   83-20553
ISBN 0-486-24610-8

Publisher's Note

Art Nouveau, the international art movement that swept Europe and America around the turn of the century, had an especially vigorous development in Germany, centered in Munich, historically the Central European mecca for artists. The magazine *Jugend* ("Youth"), subtitled "The Munich Illustrated Weekly for Art and Life," was, from its premier issue in 1896, so strongly associated with the movement in Germany that it gave its name to the style ("*Jugendstil*"). While *Jugend* was not exclusively an art journal, it was an important showcase for the graphic talents of a whole generation of artists. The decorative material that adorned its pages—frames, borders, vignettes, head- and tail-pieces and so on—has vast appeal for today's designers, illustrators, advertisers, crafts-people and others who seek authentic period graphics.

Carol Belanger Grafton has selected over 500 of the most attractive and useful graphic elements from an 18-year run of *Jugend,* sampling the work of more than 90 artists. The art is arranged in four broad categories by the dominant motif: people (pages 1–40), plants (pages 41–87), animals (pages 88–98) and abstract/geometric design (pages 99–121). Most of the art is reproduced exactly as it appeared in *Jugend.* Some designs which were originally printed in two colors or one color other than black have been converted to black and white. In a few cases, tints of gray have been substituted for areas of color to retain parts of the original design that would otherwise be lost.

Most of the designs on pages 2, 3, 5–7, 10, 14, 15, 20–24, 26–28, 30–34, 36–39, 100–102, 104 and 106–120 were taken from advertising matter that publicized a variety of goods and services. Modern commercial artists will find a wealth of useful graphics, complete with trade symbols, from which to choose.

No collection of Art Nouveau graphics would be representative of the style without images of beautiful women, and this book is replete with them. Pictures of women—classically draped, fashionably garbed in the modes of the Belle Epoque or voluptuously nude—outnumber those of men by a factor of seven. The artists of *Jugend,* like Mucha, Beardsley and many exponents of Art Nouveau in other countries, delighted in the textural possibilities of women's hair, whether loose and flowing or piled high in the coiffures of the day. The swirling lines vary infinitely, from the fine strands that form the rectangular frame at the bottom left of page 20 to the bold, silhouette-like curves that fill the mother-and-child vignette by M. Stüler-Walde on page 24. Both women and men are depicted in a wide range of activities, including dancing, cycling, painting, playing music, smoking, hunting and wooing, suggesting many new uses for the graphics.

Floral and other plant forms grow luxuriantly in these pages. Such botanically inspired designs were great favorites of the entire Art Nouveau movement, and the *Jugendstil* artists, like their French and British counterparts, made a close study of plants and their decorative applications. The familiar blossoms and foliage of garden, hothouse and pond species are well represented: roses, tulips, lupines, irises, orchids, freesias, lilies of the valley and water lilies, to name only a few. Even the humble plants of the roadside and pasture—dandelions, thistles and clover—are given interesting decorative treatment. The interpretations of floral forms contained in this book range from the academic realism of L. Kayser's lilies on page 47, with pistils, stamens and venation clearly drawn, to the geometric stylization of Wilhelm Keppler's flattened, squared-off roses on page 56.

Animal forms, though not as abundant as florals, are present in this volume in considerable number. Sea creatures, including sea horses, various other fishes and shrimps, are the basis of some appealing plates. Other compositions employ the shapes of lions, horses, cats, dogs and stags. Avian forms include those of ducks, swans, roosters, owls, pheasants and of course peacocks, in addition to an exotic emu and a pair of marabou storks. The lower orders of animal life are not neglected: frogs, snails, beetles, butterflies, moths and even caterpillars figure in the designs.

The nonfigurative material is, for the most part, composed of the undulating, "whiplash" lines that are typical of Art Nouveau. Some of it shows a tendency toward angularity, hinting at the evolution of *Jugendstil* toward its later, "constructive" variant.

A large number of the page decorations were attributed to their designers in the pages of the magazine. These identifications, most of them in the original typography, have been preserved here, and an Index of Artists appears on pages 123 and 124 (only firm attributions are indexed). Following are brief notes on the five artists whose work is most abundantly represented in the present collection, roughly in order of frequency of appearance.

Bernhard Pankok (1872–1943), a native of Münster, was trained as a sculptor, painter and restorer. He was a co-founder of the influential *Vereinigte Werkstätten für Kunst im Handwerk* ("United Workshops for Art in Handicraft"), a frequent design contributor to *Jugend* and also to the important Berlin-based art journal *Pan,* and the director of the State Arts and Crafts School in Stuttgart for nearly 25 years.

Otto Eckmann (1865–1902), a versatile graphic designer, craftsman and painter who is probably the best known of the Munich group, was born in Hamburg. A brilliant interpreter of floral forms, Eckmann was, early in his career, a Symbolist painter of some note. He later designed one of the most important *Jugendstil* typefaces ("Eckmann-Schrift"), settings of which appear in the captions on pages 47, 79, 93 and 97.

Hans Christiansen (1866–1945), born in Flensburg near the Danish border, was associated with the Darmstadt artists' colony (a secondary center of German Art Nouveau) for several years, and achieved special distinction as a textile designer. Nuremberg-born Julius Diez, one of the few native Bavarians represented here, studied, worked and taught in Munich for most of his long life. Many of the designs by the short-lived Bostonian painter, designer and etcher George Ernst Dodge (1863–1898) were published posthumously. (His first initial is occasionally misquoted as "C." in the captions.)

Of the other artists, whose work is represented by fewer than ten designs in this book, special mention should be made of Peter Behrens (1868–1940), a leader of the Munich Secession; Fritz Hellmut Ehmcke (b. 1878), whose *Graphic Trade Symbols by German Designers* has been published by Dover (1974, 21671-3); Fritz Erler (1868–1940), a co-founder of *Jugend;* Ludwig Hohlwein (1874–1949), a major poster artist (45 of his works are reproduced in *Hohlwein Posters in Full Color* [Dover, 1976, 23408-8]); Bruno Paul (1874–1968), active in architecture and interior design as well as graphics; Ferdinand Freiherr von Reznicek (1868–1909), an illustrator of noble birth; and Emil Rudolf Weiss (1875–1942), an important type designer. (Further information about many *Jugendstil* artists is available in Michael Weisser's *Im Stil der "Jugend"* [Frankfurt, Verlag Dieter Fricke, 1979] and Hans H. Hofstätter's *Jugendstil Druckkunst* [Baden-Baden, Holle-Verlag, 1968], both sources for this note.)

J. R. Witzel

Fritz Dannenberg

F. v. Reznicek

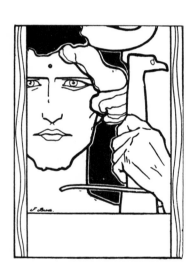

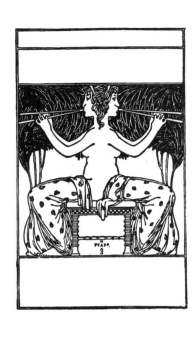

Julius Diez

Fritz Erler

Chr. Wild.

Fidus

Fritz Erler.

Anna Hanfing

A. Hartung

H. Goltz.

E. M. Lilien.

Fidus.

E. Everbeck

6

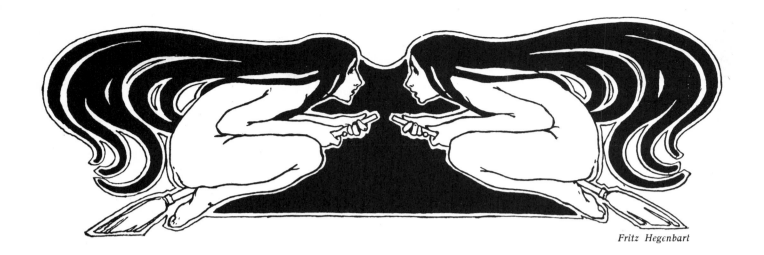

Fritz Hegenbart

Fritz Erler

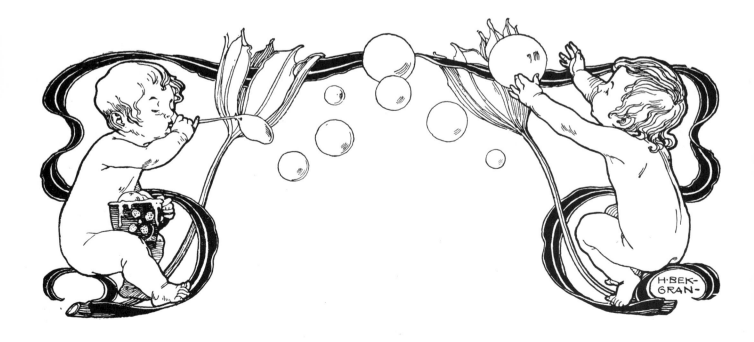

Fidus

Chr. Wild.

H. Meyer-Cassel

A. Fiebiger

Pankok.

Minna Lowy

Josef Rudolf Witzel

Haas

Walter Püttner

Hans Pfaff

Fritz Erler

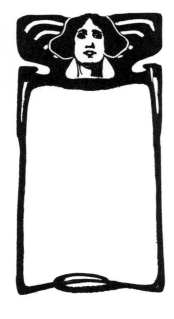

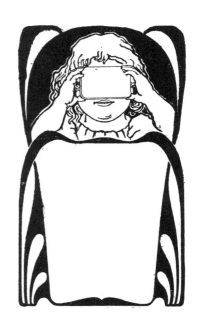

A. Schmidhammer

— Fidus —

H. Bek-Gran

Max Feldbauer

15

H. Eichrodt

Hans Eichrodt

H. Eichrodt

Franz Christophe

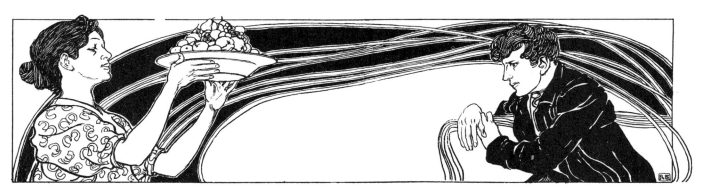

Robert Engels

Josef Rudolf Witzel

R. Eddelbüttel.

E. Ewerbeck.

M. Stüler-Walde.

Christiansen

P. Fliegner

G. E. Dodge

J. R. Witzel

E. Neumann

FRAV MVSICA · CASPARI·

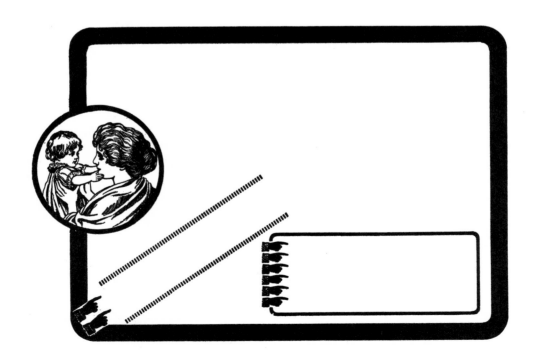

Fritz Erler

Fritz Erler.

Jul. Diez

Fritz Erler

29

Hans Christiansen

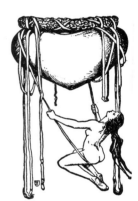

Fidus

Fidus

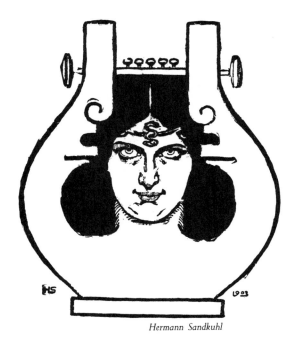

Hermann Sandkuhl

Chr. Wild

J. R. Witzel

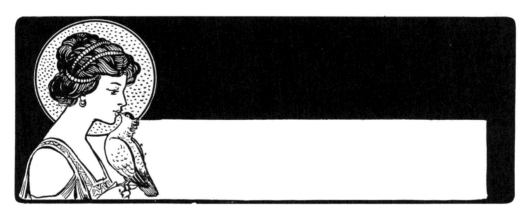

Josef Rudolf Witzel

CASPARI

E KUTHAN

J. R. Witzel

Léon Ruffé.

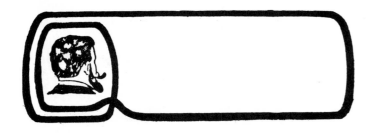

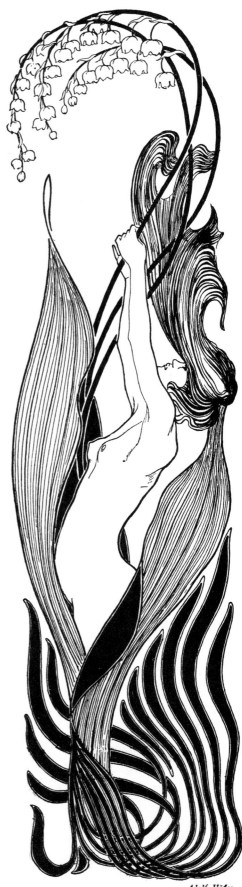

J. Diez

Adolf Höfer

Bruno Paul

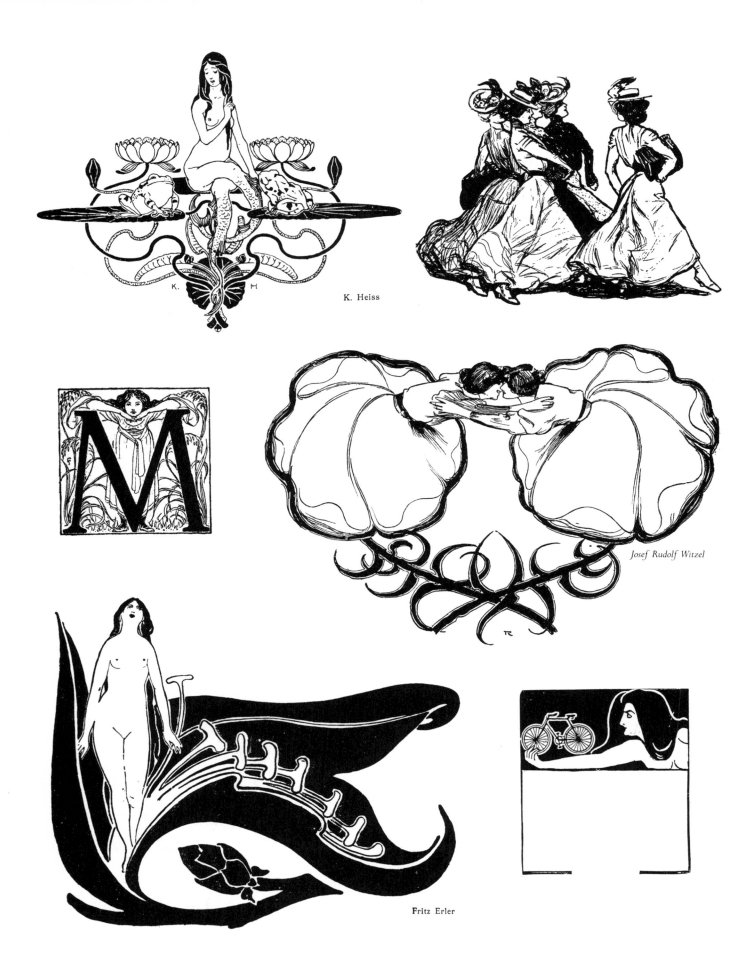

K. Heiss

Josef Rudolf Witzel

Fritz Erler

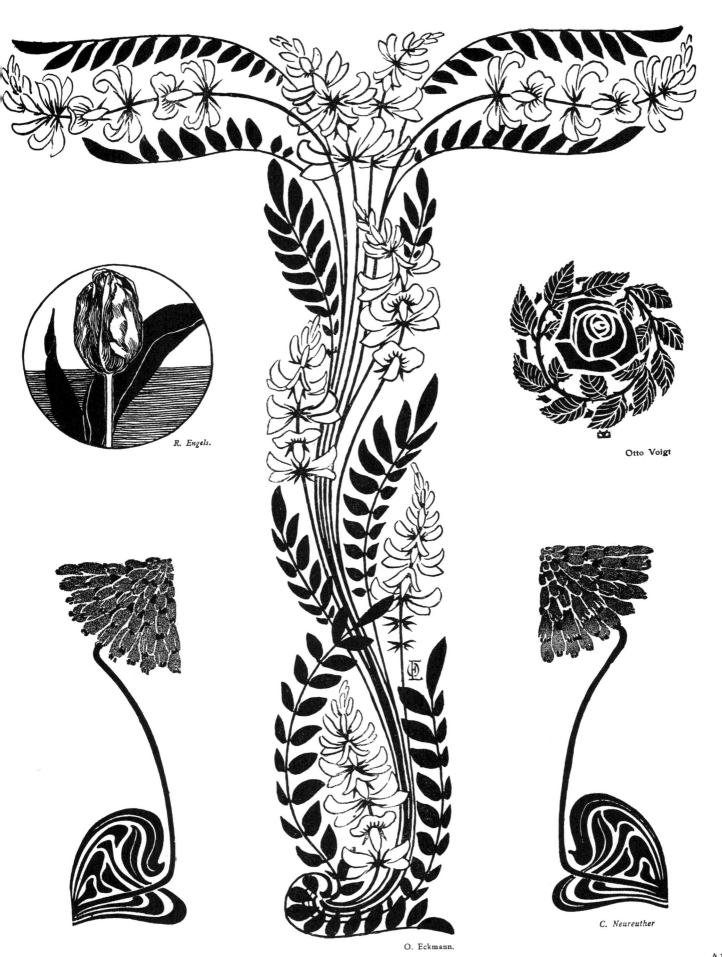

R. Engels.

Otto Voigt

O. Eckmann.

C. Neureuther

41

P. Haustein

G. Petzoldt

42

Hans Christiansen

Gustav Petzoldt

43

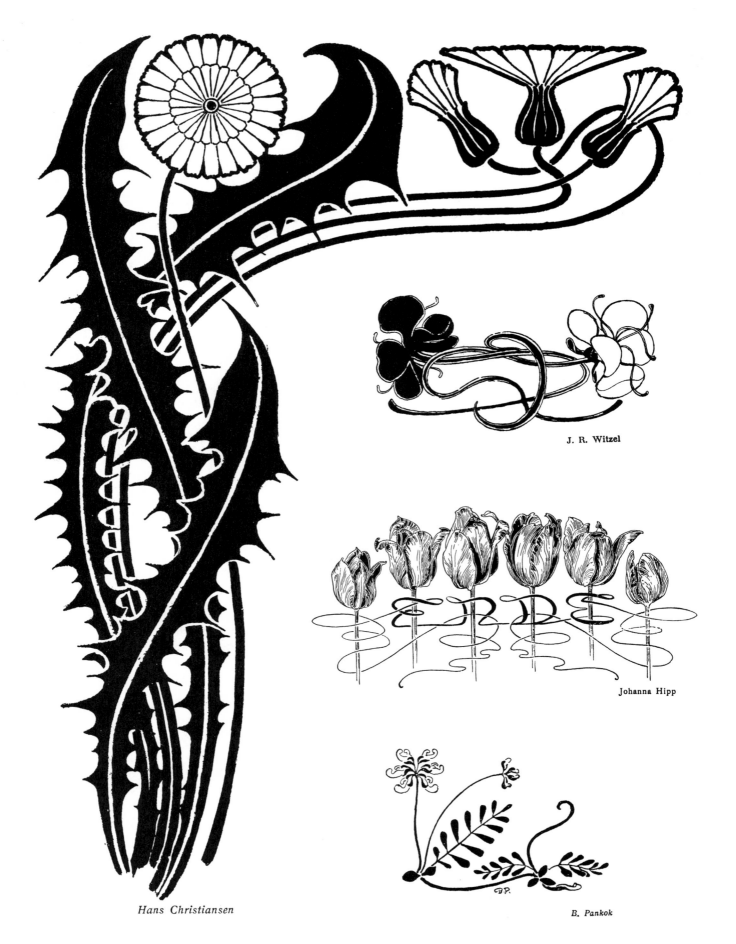

Hans Christiansen

J. R. Witzel

Johanna Hipp

B. Pankok

44

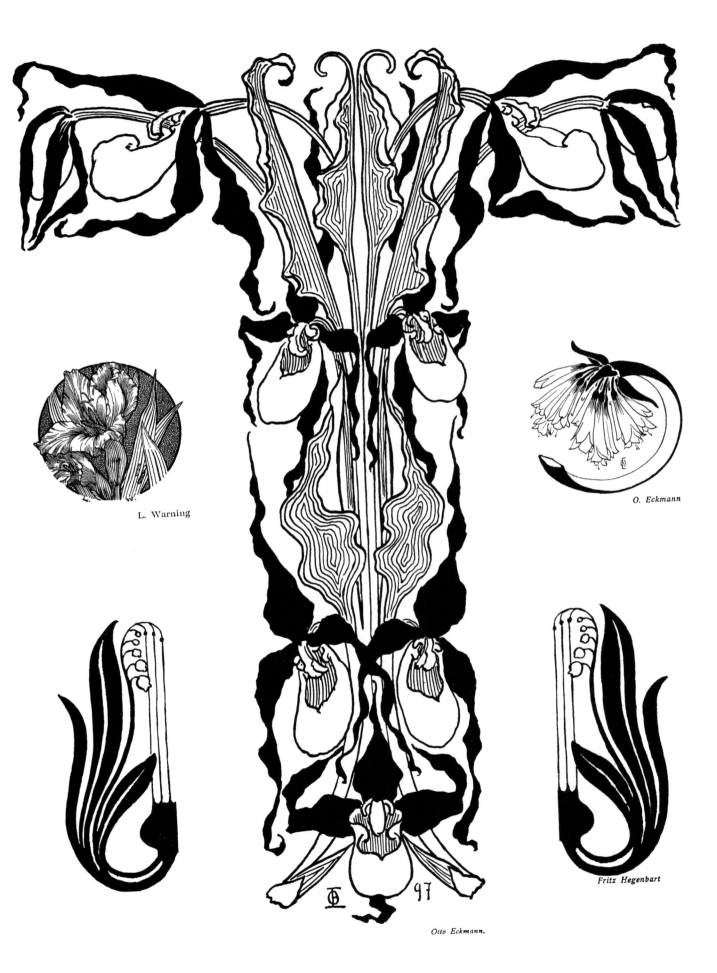

L. Warning

O. Eckmann

Fritz Hegenbart

Otto Eckmann.

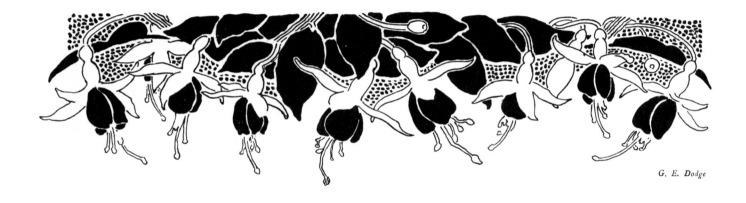

G. E. Dodge

P. Haustein

46

Emil Schuller

L. Kayser.

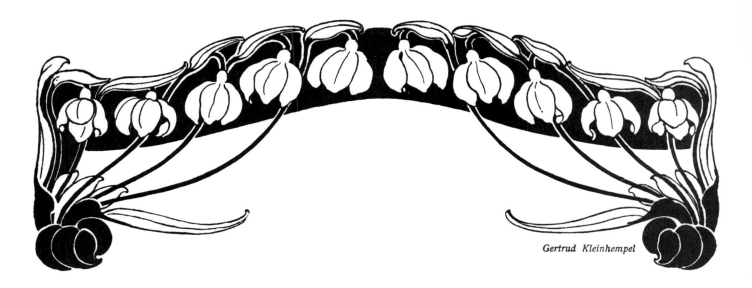

Gertrud Kleinhempel

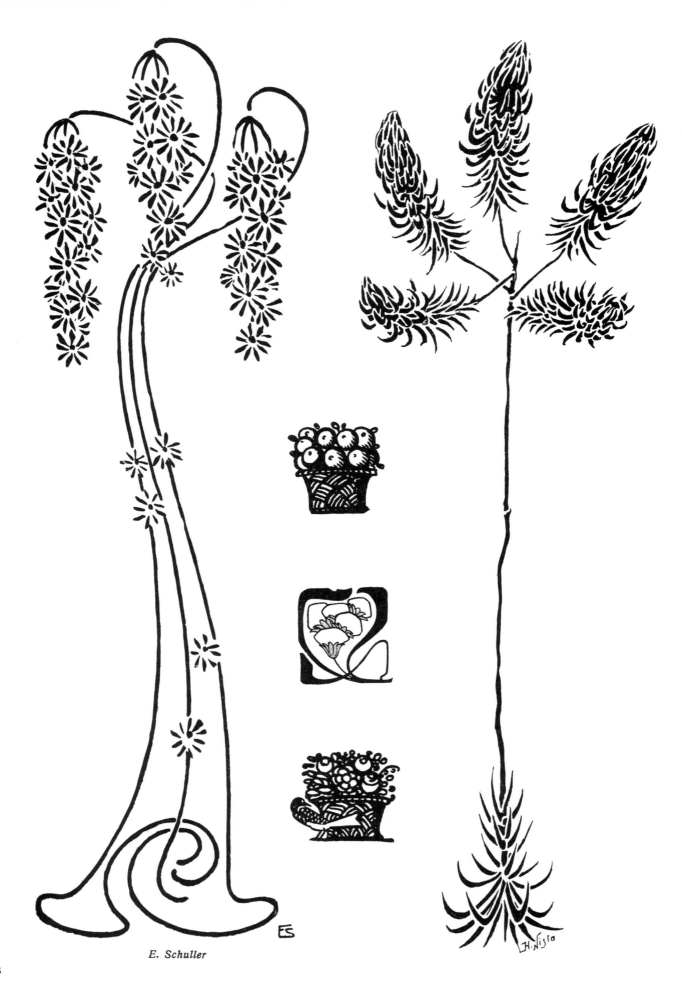

E. Schuller

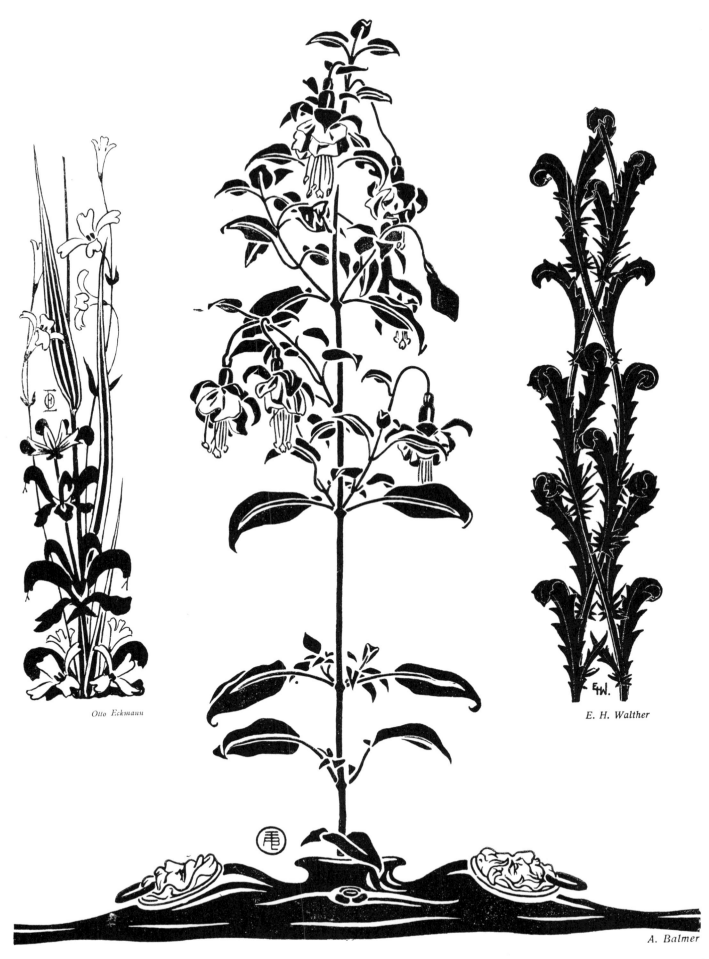

Otto Eckmann

E. H. Walther

A. Balmer

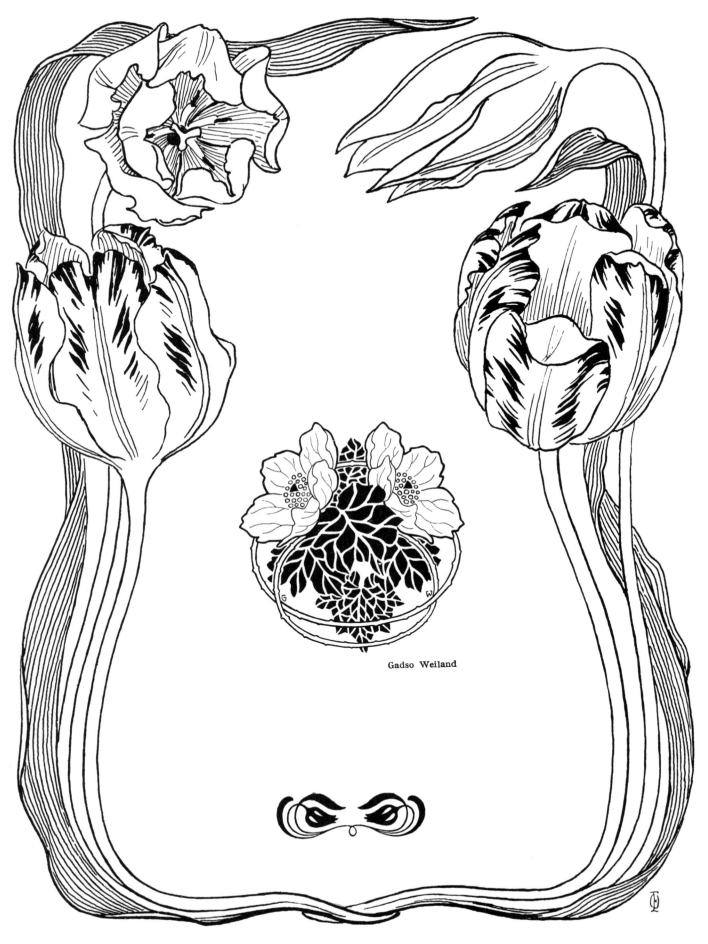

Gadso Weiland

50

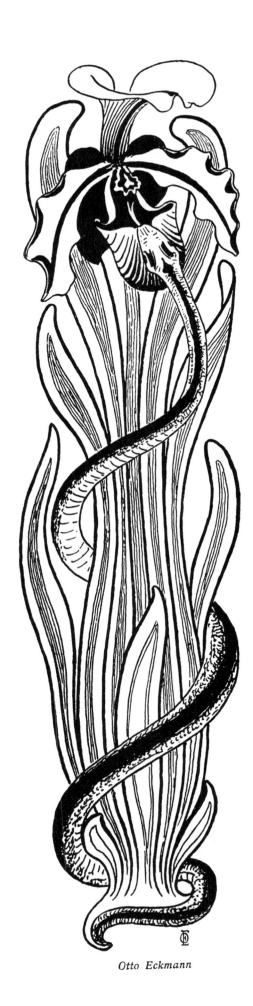

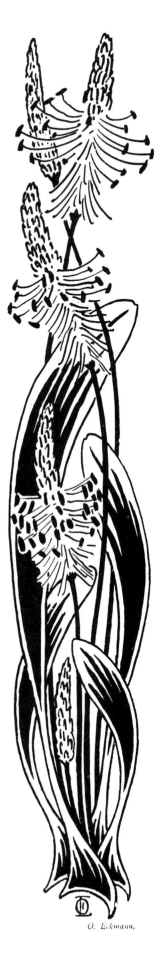

CASPARI.

Otto Eckmann

O. Eckmann.

H. Nisle

Julius Diez

A. Weisgerber

E. L. Fuchs

C. Neureuther

Gertrud Kleinhempel

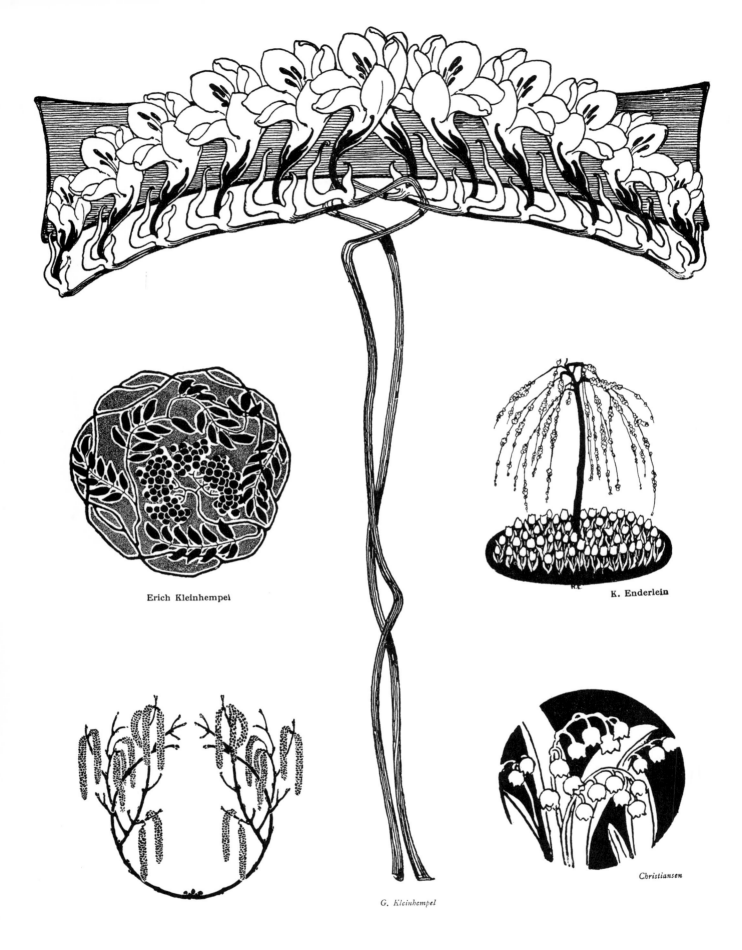

Erich Kleinhempel

K. Enderlein

G. Kleinhempel

Christiansen

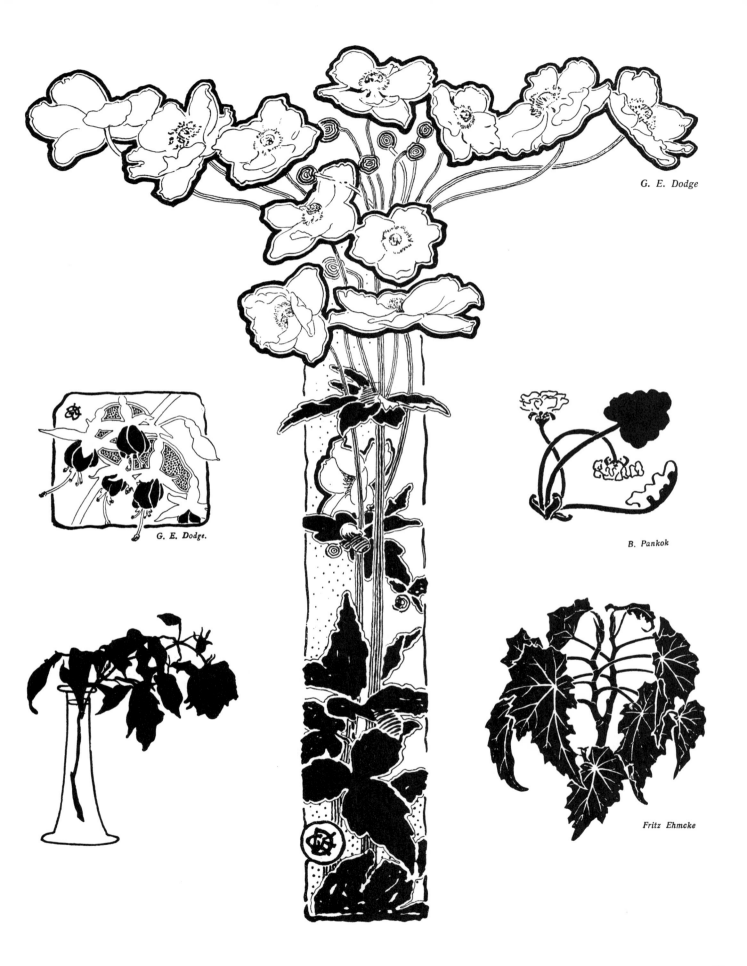

G. E. Dodge

G. E. Dodge.

B. Pankok

Fritz Ehmcke

55

C. E. Dodge

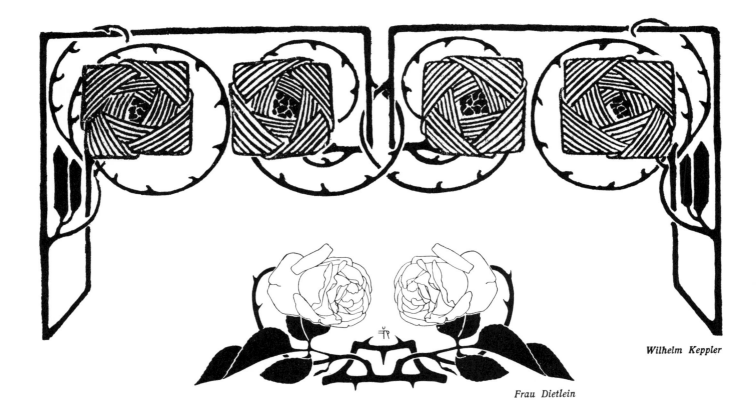

Wilhelm Keppler

Frau Dietlein

Ernst Vollbehr

56

O. Eckmann.

Hans Christiansen

G. E. Dodge

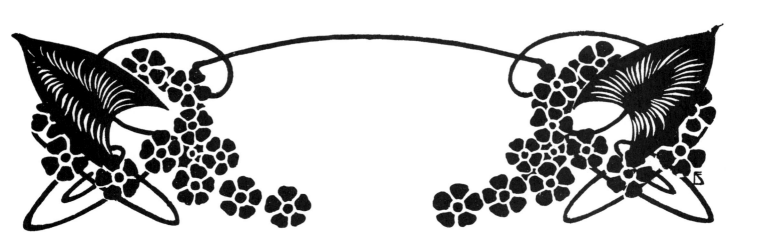

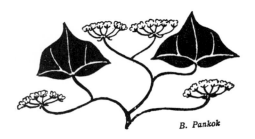

B. Pankok

Fritz Erler

P. Huber

58

H. Goltz

Bernhard Pankok

H. Christiansen

Otto Eckmann.

B. Pankok

F. Hegenbart

P. Haustein

61

B. Pankok.

B. Pankok.

Hans Christiansen

O. Eckmann.

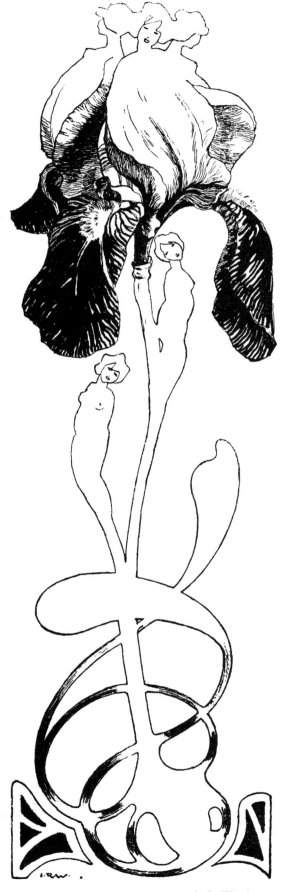

J. R. Witzel.

Jul. Diez

Gertrud Kleinhempel

M. v. Brauchitsch

G. Weiland

F. W. NEUMEYER

65

Elise Schill

Gertrud Kleinhempel

G. E. Dodge

Johanna Hipp

P. Haustein

G. E. Dodge

Gertrud Kleinhempel

Meyer-Nicolai

F. Hegenbart

H. Christiansen

E. Volbehr

E. Everbeck

Emil Spatz

69

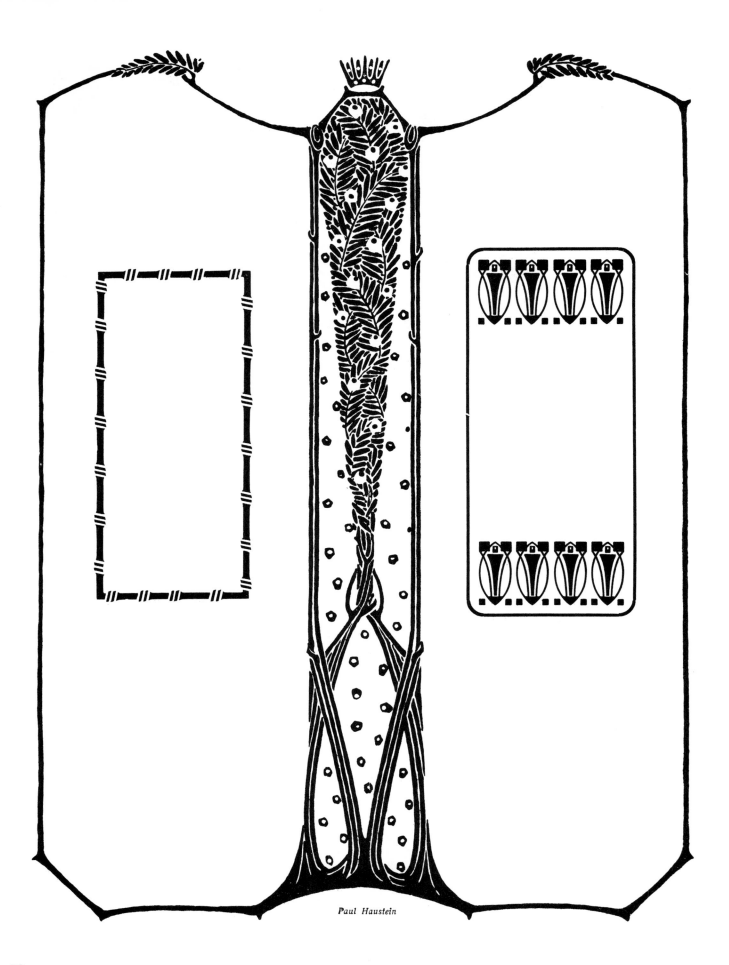

Paul Haustein

H. Christiansen

P. Haustein

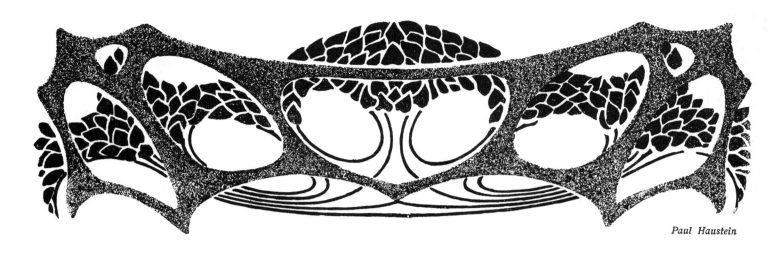

Paul Haustein

E. Schuller

Gadso Weiland

C. E. Dodge

E. Schuller

Gertrud Kleinhempel

73

H. Meyer-Cassel

Bernhard Pankok

74

G. Petzoldt

P. Fliegner

75

Frau Dietlein

B. Pankok

Hans Christiansen

Margarethe v. Brauchitsch

G. E. Dodge

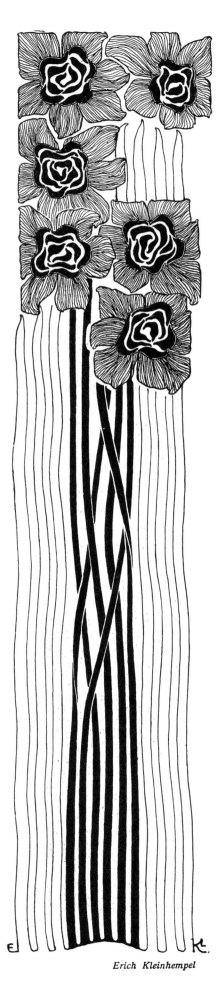

Erich Kleinhempel

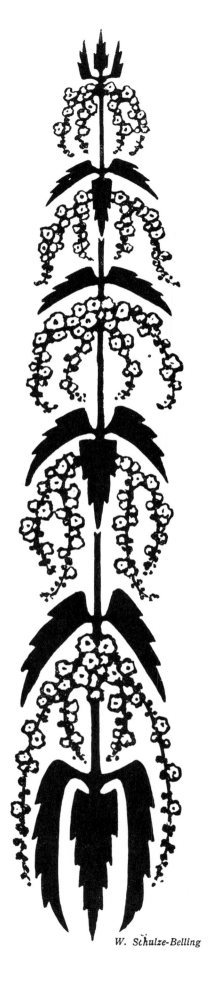

W. Schulze-Belling

G. Petzoldt

— E. Schuller —

Hans Christiansen

Peter Bauer

B Pankok

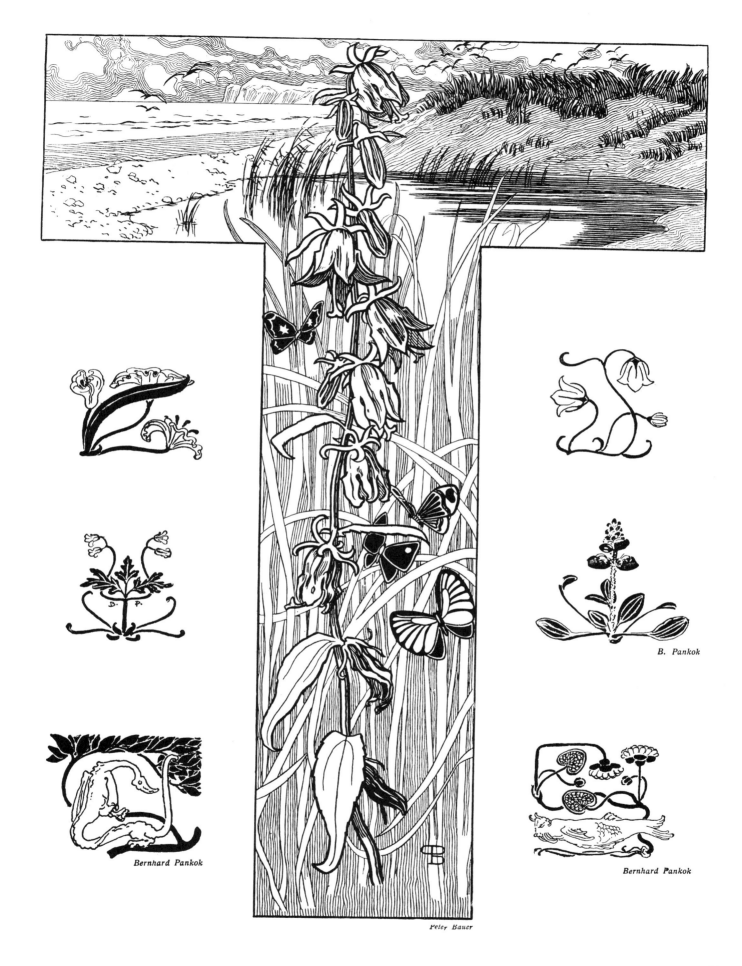

Bernhard Pankok

B. Pankok

Bernhard Pankok

Peter Bauer

G. Weiland

F. Steiniger

Fritz Hellmut Ehmcke

H. Goltz

J. Lichtenberg

E. M. Lilien

(Chr. Neureuther)

Gertrud Kleinhempel

Fritz Scherz

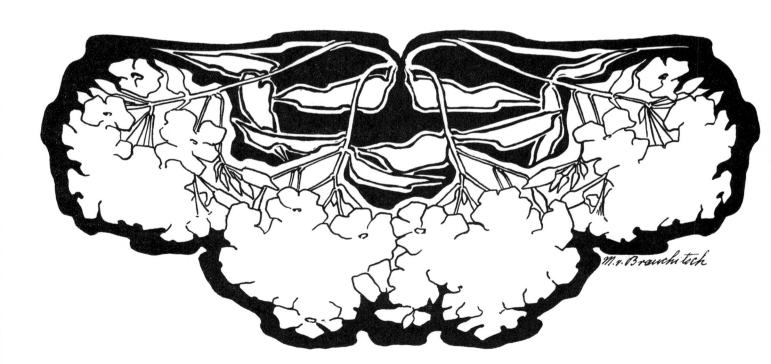

M. v. Brauchitsch

Otto Eckmann

Meyer-Cassel

Meyer-Nicolai

F. Meyner

H. Goltz

H. Nisle

A. Balmer

Franz Christophe

J. Berchthold.

pupil of Otto Eckmann

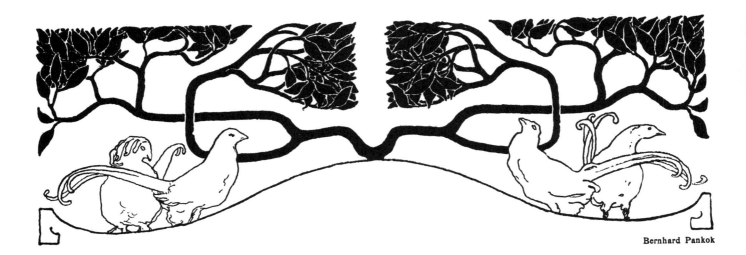

Bernhard Pankok

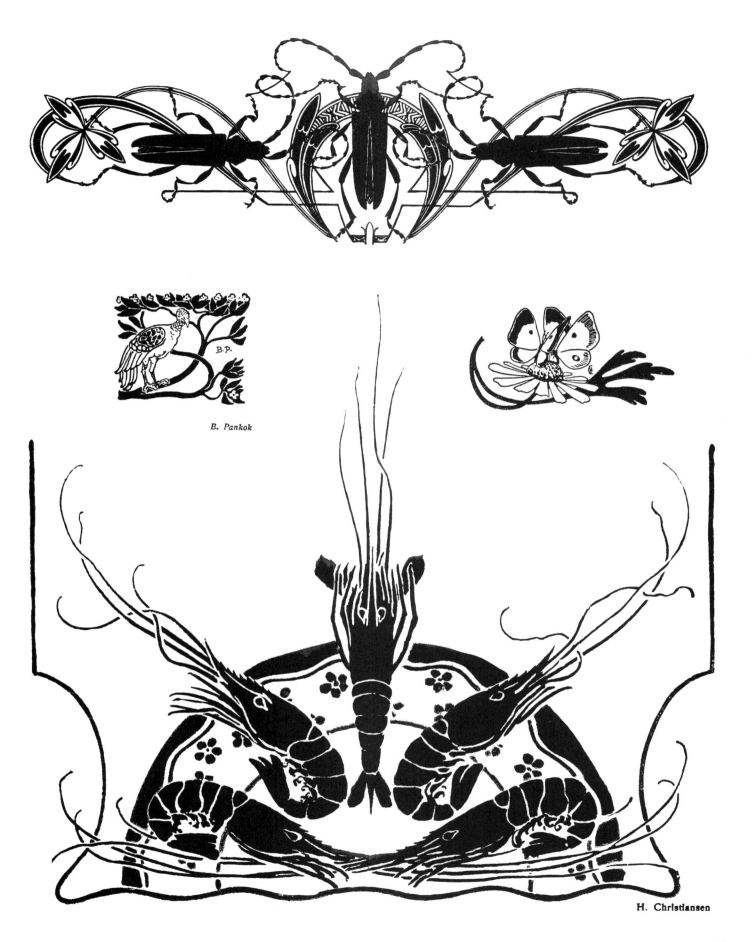

B. Pankok

H. Christiansen

Bernhard Pankok

Franz Christophe

Fritz Erler

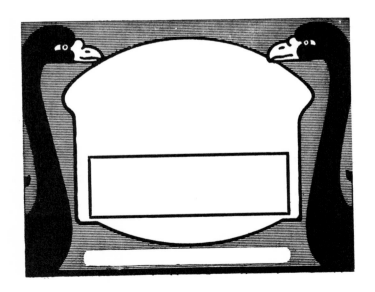

H. Wittig

B. Pankok

E. Tönnies

91

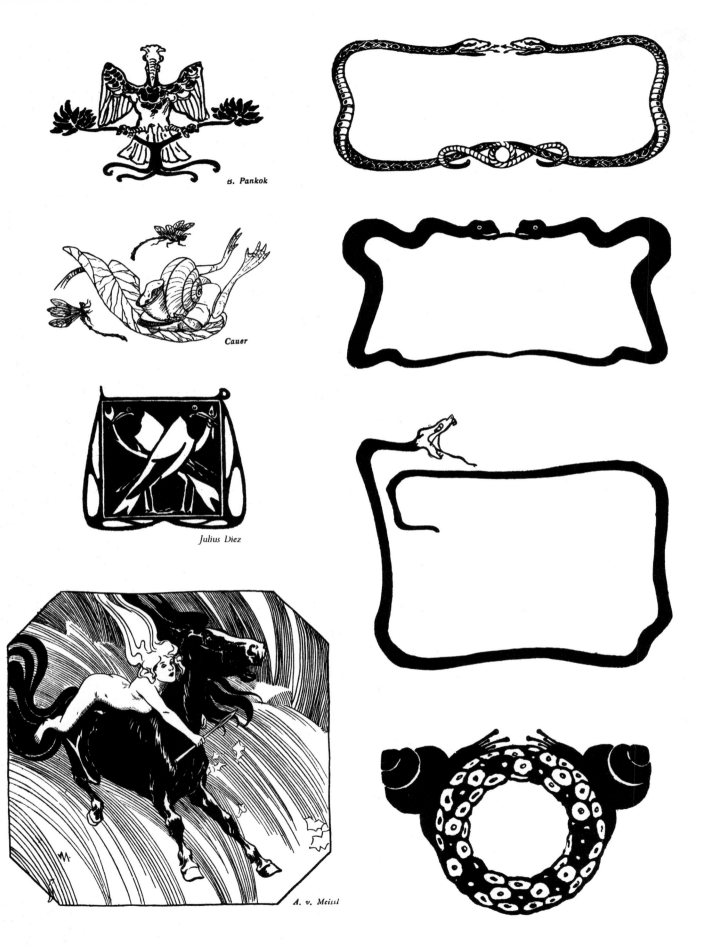

B. Pankok

Cauer

Julius Diez

A. v. Meissl

Julius Diez

H. Nisle

Jul. Diez

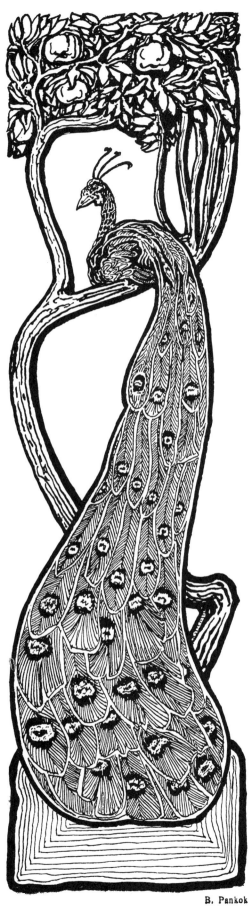

B. Pankok

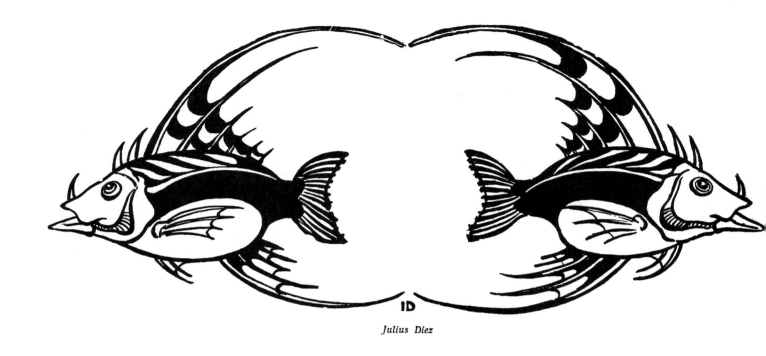

Julius Diez

Ludwig Hohlwein

J. Diez.

Fritz Hegenbart

Max Wislicenus

Ludwig Hohlwein

Albert Weisgerber

Julius Diez

Julius Diez

J. Gerstmann

B. Pankok.

J. Gerstmann

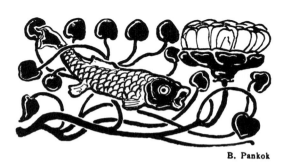

B. Pankok

CARL SCHM.-HTS.

F. Christophe

C. Schmidt-Helmbrechts.

R. Bossert

Otto Eckmann

F. Hegenbart

B. Panitz.

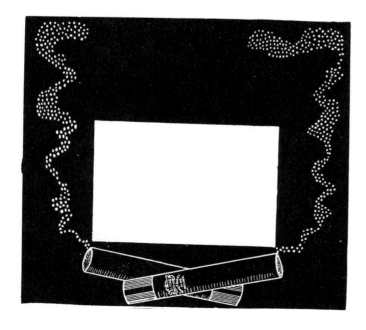

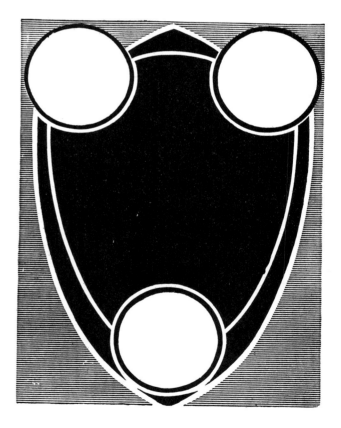

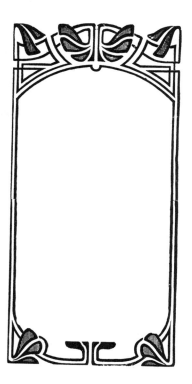

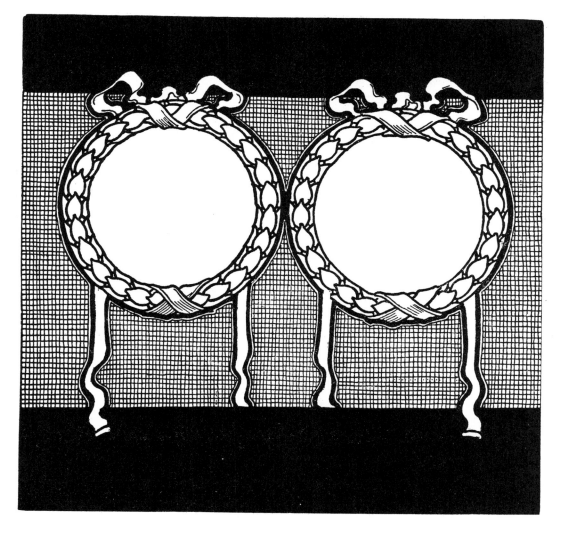

Otto Eckmann

O. Eckmann

O. Eckmann

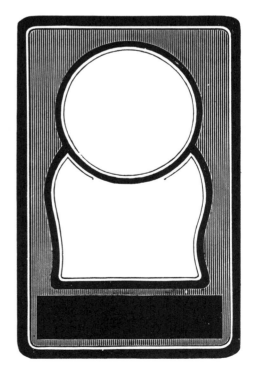

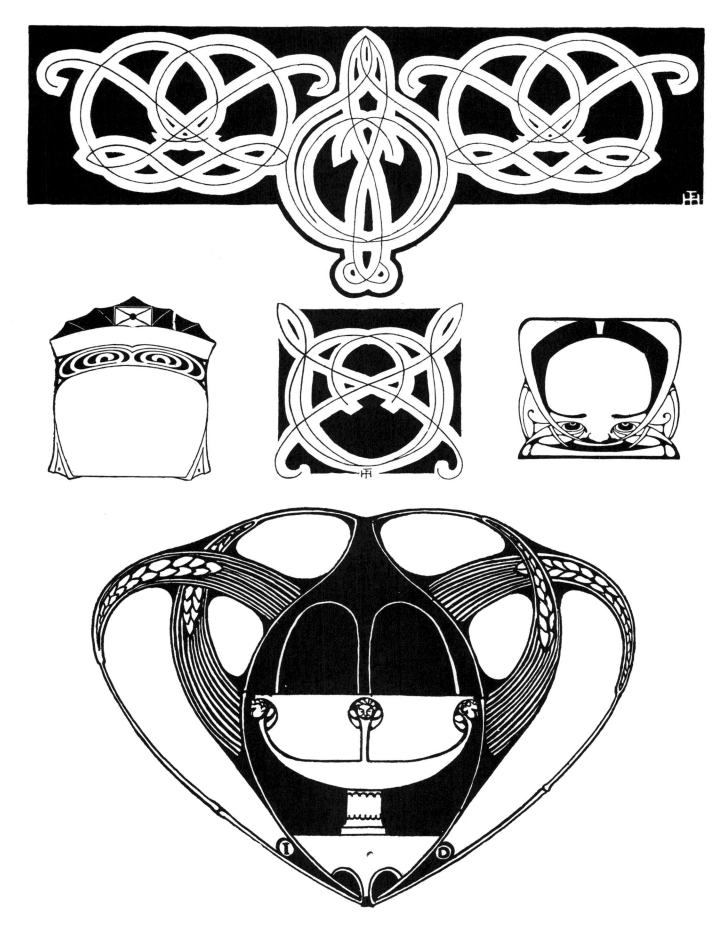

A. Martini.

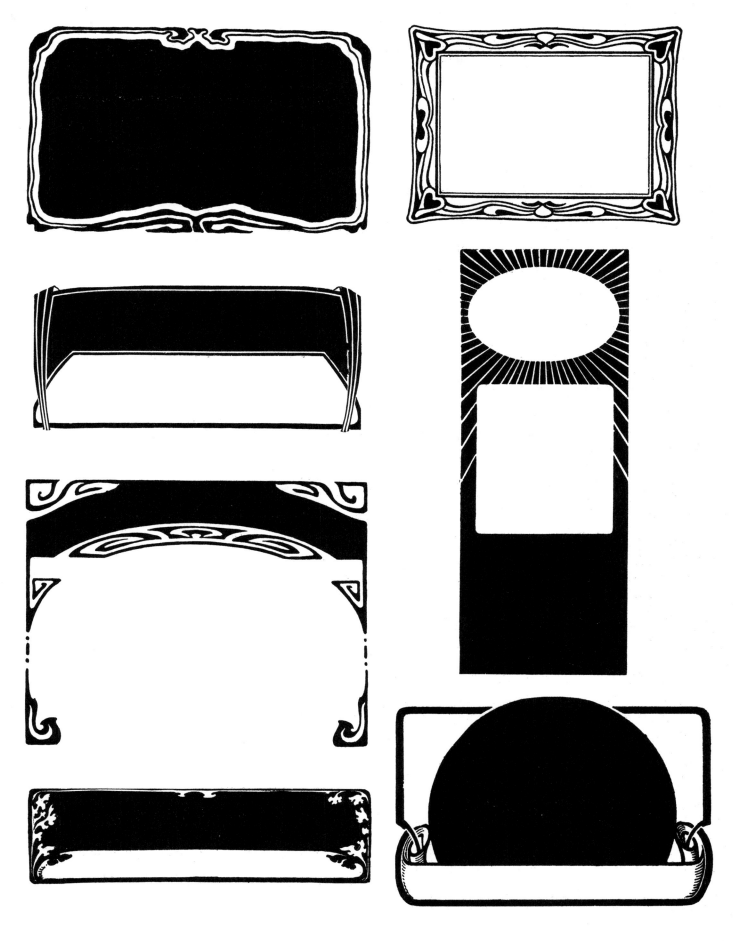

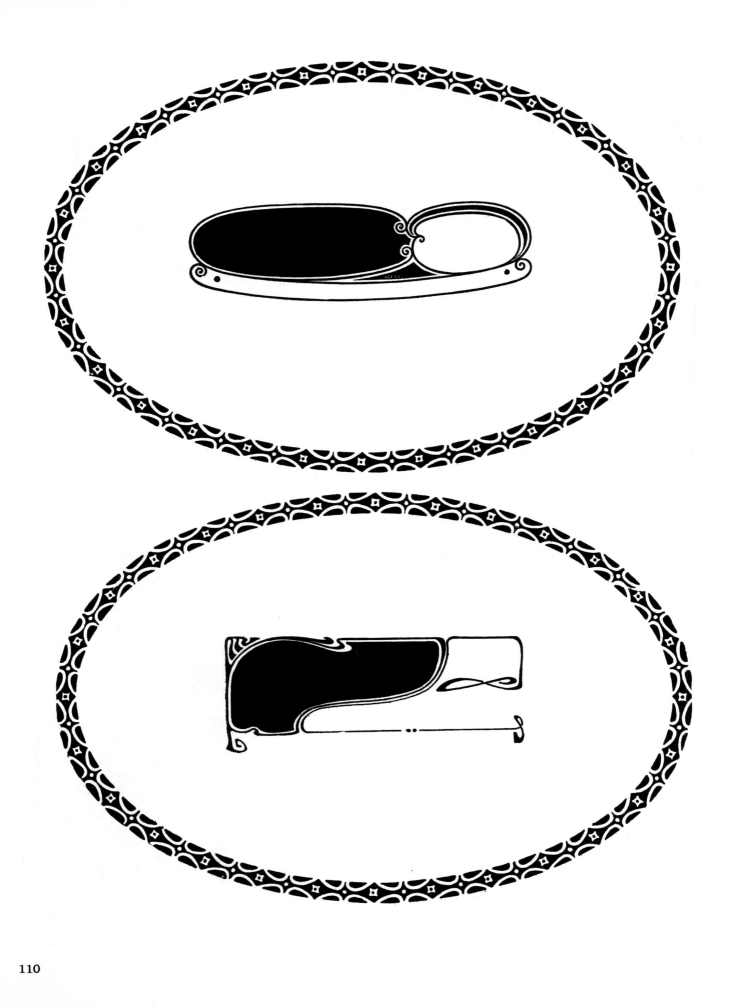

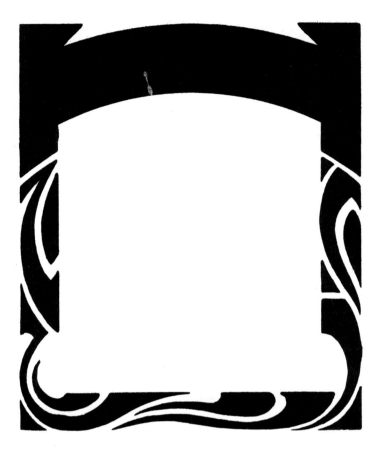

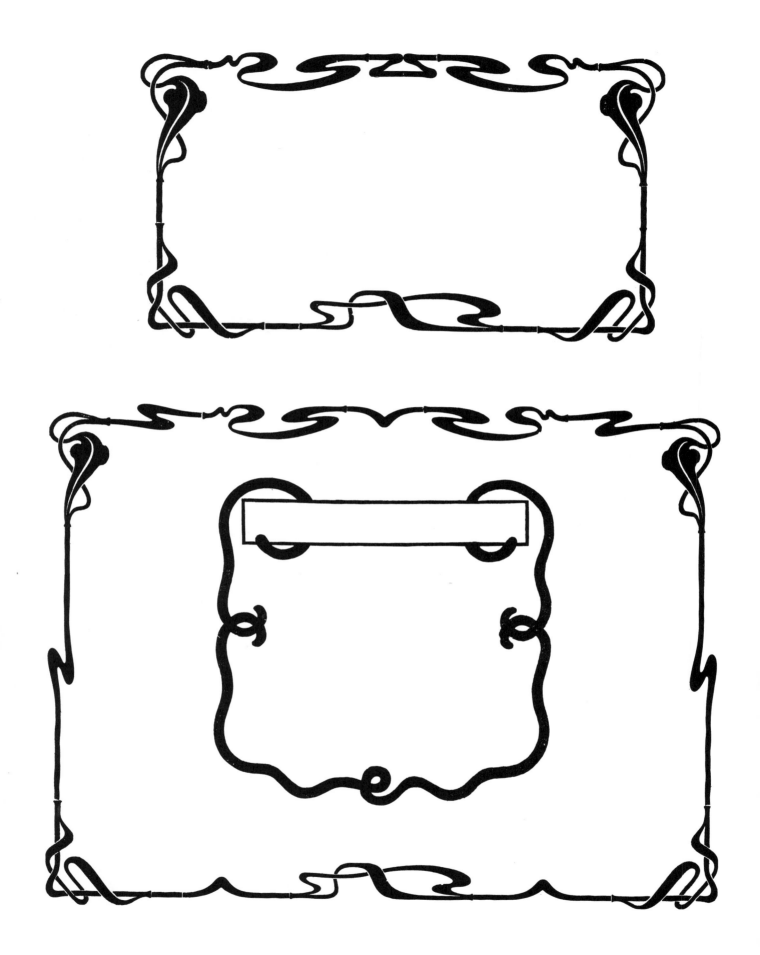

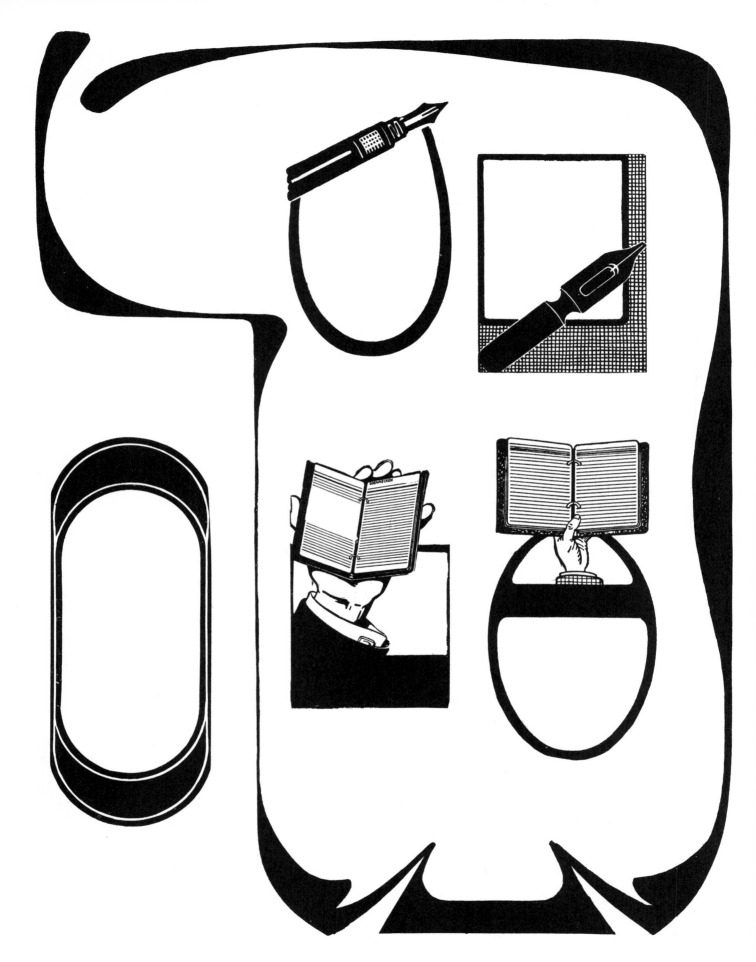

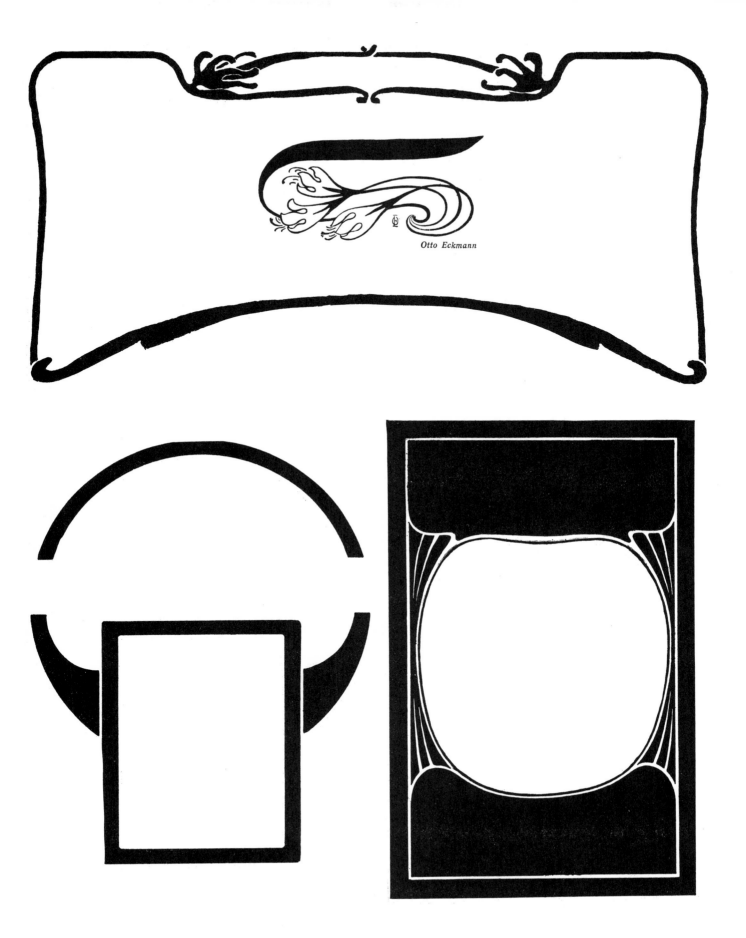

Otto Eckmann

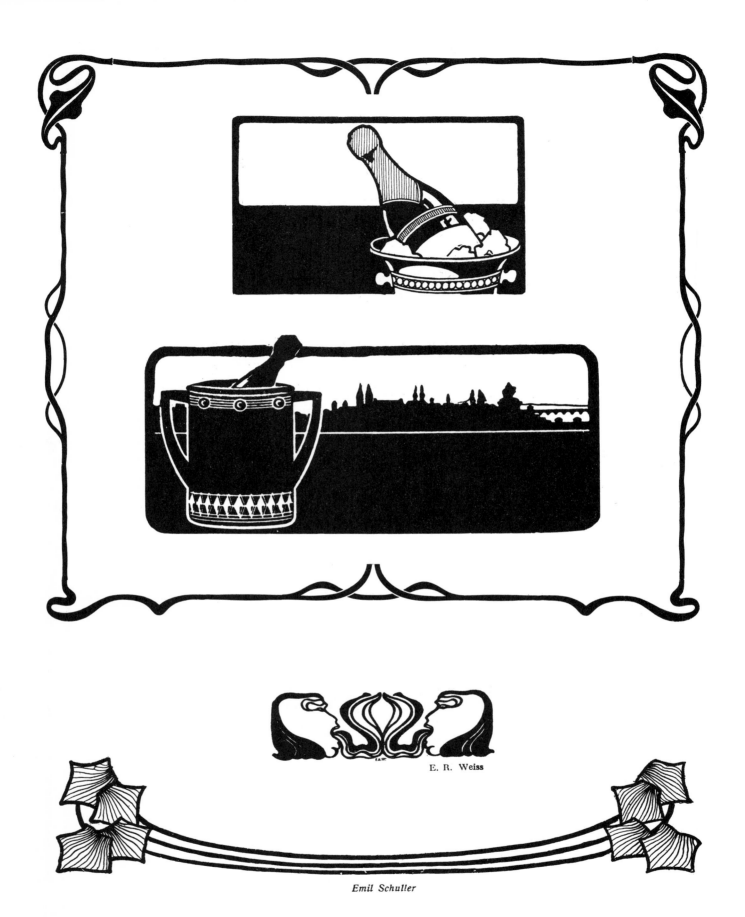

E. R. Weiss

Emil Schuller

Peter Behrens

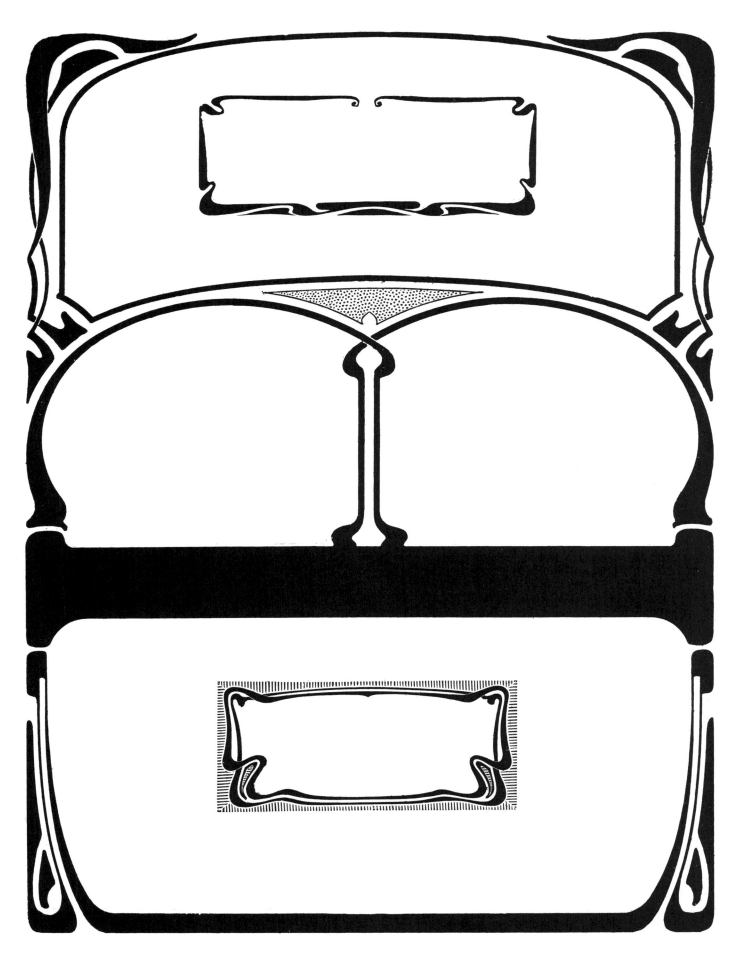

INDEX OF ARTISTS

Only firm attributions are indexed.